Plants and Seeds

Written by Cindy Barden
Illustrated by Nancee McClure

Most plants, like trees,
grow from seeds.

So do flowers,

and so do weeds.

Planting a garden

can be lots of fun.

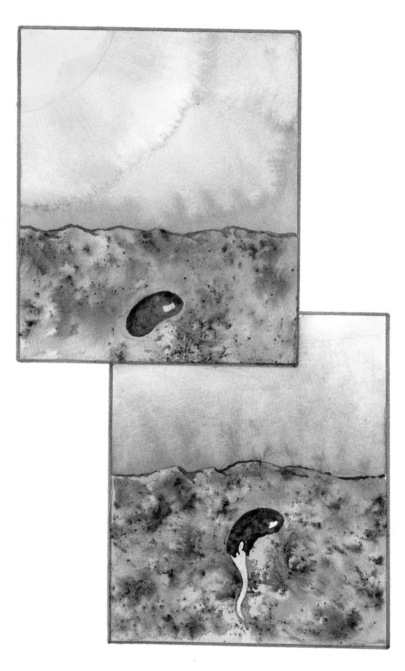

The seeds need good soil,

water, and sun.

Now the plants
begin to grow

stems above the ground
and roots below.

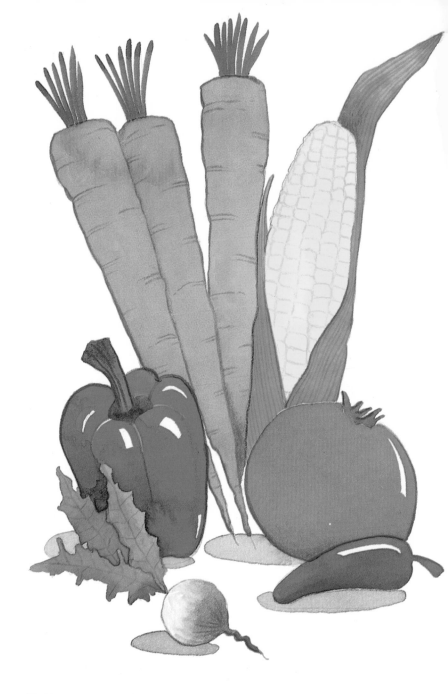

Many plants are good to eat.

**Fruits and berries
taste quite sweet.**

Big plants and small plants,

flowers and trees,

**bushes and vines;
they all grow from seeds.**